Eat
Your
Colors!

Terry Harris

Terry Harris

LifeRich Publishing books may be ordered through booksellers or by contacting:

LifeRich Publishing
1663 Liberty Drive
Bloomington, IN 47403
www.liferichpublishing.com
1 (888) 238-8637

ISBN: 978-1-4897-0187-9 (sc)
ISBN: 978-1-4897-0186-2 (hc)
ISBN: 978-1-4897-0188-6 (e)

Printed in the United States of America.

LifeRich Publishing rev. date: 4/22/2014

To my grandchildren Madison and Logan,
for whom this book was written.
I love them with all my heart.

Eat colors, said your mommy,
They are so good for you.
Eat the red and green and yellow,
And even eat the blue!

The berries are so tasty,
The squash and peppers, too,
The apples are real yummy,
Grapes and plums are good for you!

Eating colors is so funny,
We love them every day.
When you eat up all your colors
So healthy you will stay!

Fun Food Faces!

Eat Red!

Red is red, and when I'm fed,
I love to be fed a tasty red.
Red is apples, juicy and sweet,
Cherries and berries are yummy treats,
Red tomatoes and peppers, too,
Which ones can I give to you?
Watermelon is my favorite red,
But I can't eat it when I stand on my head!

Apple

Cherries

Strawberries

Raspberries

Tomato

Pepper

Watermelon

Orange is so bright and sassy,
Lots of foods are really classy.
A pumpkin ready for Halloween,
A peach fit for a king and queen,
Sweet potatoes, an orange treat,
Oranges and cantaloupe taste so sweet.
Carrots do make a tasty dinner,
And apricots for dessert are a winner!

Pumpkin

Peach

Sweet potatoes

Orange

Cantaloupe

Carrots

Apricots

Eat Yellow!

Yellow is yellow, soft and mellow,
Yellow for this hungry fellow.
Yellow corn is good to eat,
And squash, a sunny yellow treat.
Bananas, pears and pineapple, too;
They are all so good for you.
Grapefruit and lemons, tangy, tangy,
Make my mouth feel twangy, twangy!

Corn

Squash

Bananas

Pear

Pineapple

Grapefruit

Lemons

Eat Green!

Green is green, and I'm not mean
When eating foods that are green.
Broccoli looks like a great big tree,
Kiwi is so delicious to me;
String beans and peas a favorite green,
And meet zucchini on the scene.
Asparagus and celery with tops so wispy,
A yummy salad with lettuce crispy;
Green pepper is so good to eat
And green cucumber, a tasty treat!

Broccoli

Kiwi

String beans

Peas

Zucchini

Lettuce

Asparagus

Celery

Green pepper

Cucumber

Eat Blue and Purple!

Purple and blue are foods so yummy,
I love to put them in my tummy.
Purple plums and purple grapes,
I wonder if they're loved by apes.
Purple eggplant is not an egg at all,
And purple cabbage is shaped like a ball.
Blue I love, but there's only one,
Blueberries, blueberries, oh so fun!

Blueberries

Plums

Grapes

Eggplant

Cabbage

Eat White!

White is white, no color in sight
But here are white foods that I like.
A cup of milk, my favorite drink,
Yummy yogurt, ready in a wink,
Mushrooms are a funny little food,
But they taste really oh, so good!
Cauliflower is not really a flower,
But white foods give me lots of power!

Milk

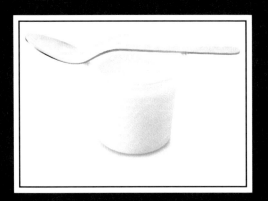

Yogurt

Mushrooms

Cauliflower

Eat Brown!

Brown foods really aren't too many;
Can you look around and find any?
Brown nuts are really delightful and fun,
Almonds and cashews and peanuts, yum!
Potatoes with wonderful skin that is brown,
Some are long and some are round.
Beans, my favorite brown food today;
I'll eat them before I go out and play!

Nuts

Potatoes

Beans

So many colors everywhere
In foods we eat each day;
Eating many colors
Gives us energy as we play.

Count your colors every day,
Count them one by one.
Fill your plate with colors
To have a lot of fun!

Can you find the colors?

Can you find the red tomato?

Can you find the white mushrooms?

Can you find the green cucumber?

Can you find the red pepper?

Can you find the brown potatoes?

Can you find the orange carrots?

Can you find the green lettuce?

Can you find the foods?

Can you find the green zucchini?

Can you find the purple plums?

Can you find the red watermelon?

Can you find the white cauliflower?

Can you find the red raspberries?

Can you find the green pepper?

Can you find the yellow bananas?

Can you find the purple eggplant?

Can you find the orange carrots?

We love to eat our colors!